THE
COUNTRY NOTE-BOOK

An illustrated journal with space for notes

April in New England is like first love.

— GLADYS TABER (1899–1980)
American author

Frogs croak in the night. It is a sound we learn to live without in the city, but it can instantly summon a flood of memories of a country childhood.

— THE NATIONAL GEOGRAPHIC SOCIETY *(founded 1888)*

In the country you need to notice things.

— JOHN GRAVES, b. 1920
American writer

The word neighbor, when used by people living in the city, has a transplanted sound . . . in the truer sense of the term, neighbors are indigenous to the country.

— WALTER A. DYER (1878–1943)
American writer

It may be life, but ain't it slow?

— A. P. HERBERT *(1890–1971)*
American writer

Most of us who go to the country from a city background have some nostalgia for the old ways, even if it only manifests itself in a wagonwheel hung over the gate and an expensive fieldstone fireplace and a delux edition of *Walden* on the coffee table.

— JOHN GRAVES, b. 1920
American writer

They too were escaping from town, to live naturally, in a rich blend of savagery and philosophy.

— E. B. WHITE, b. 1899
American writer

The weekend world is a modern invention. You didn't need a weekend to get to the country in Ezra's day; the country then reached right into the backyards of the cities—the cities, indeed, were mere villages.

— LEWIS GANNIT, *b. 1891*
American writer

When we depend less on industrially produced consumer goods, we can live in quiet places. Our bodies become vigorous; we discover the serenity of living with the rhythms of the earth. We cease oppressing one another.

— ALICIA BAY LAUREL, b. 1949
American naturalist

When I am in the country I wish to vegetate like the country.
— WILLIAM HAZLITT (1778–1830)
British essayist

I like trees because they seem more resigned to the way they have to live than other things do.

— WILLA CATHER (1873–1947)
American writer

It takes courage to just up and say you don't like the country. Everybody likes the country.

— LILLIAN HELLMAN, *b. 1906*
American writer

There's something solid and reassuring about a civilization when a horse stops at a brimming trough, plunges his head into the clear, cold water, and blows and snorts in unmistakable satisfaction.

— HAYDN S. PEARSON, b. 1910
American naturalist

All it takes to be a successful farmer these days is faith, hope and parity.

— EVAN ESAR, b. 1899
American humorist

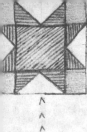

The diligent farmer plants trees, of which he himself will never see the fruit.

— CICERO (106 B.C.–43 B.C.)
Roman statesman, writer

There's no doubt about it, summer in the country is restful, even relaxing—for visitors. Not for those who live here the year around.

— HAL BORLAND (1900–1978)
American writer

To dig and delve in nice clean dirt
Can do a mortal little hurt.

— JOHN KENDRICK BANGS, b. 1933
American writer

Today one small, well-kept farm, even if only a couple of acres, is worth a thousand cars spilling off the General Motors assembly line.

— RICHARD W. LANGER, b. 1935
American writer

As a boy on a farm in Canada, I had to help move great tonnages of this nutrient every spring. Nothing is so nostalgic as that odour—in combination with the knowledge that someone else is doing the shoveling.

— JOHN KENNETH GALBRAITH, b. 1908
Canadian-born economist

There is something frank and joyous and young in the open face of the country. It gives itself ungrudgingly to the moods of the season, holding nothing back.

— WILLA CATHER (1873–1947)
American writer

I hate the country's dirt and manners, yet I love the silence; I embrace the wit.

— WILLIAM HABINGTON (1605–1664)
British poet

Cursing the weather is bad farming.

— J. C. BRIDGE (1884–1943)
American author

Perhaps not since the fall of Babylon have so many city dwellers wanted to "return" to the country without ever having been there in the first place.

— RICHARD W. LANGER, b. 1935
American writer

One of the pleasant things about living in the country is that there aren't any holidays. One day is like the next and if you want a day off you can take it when you like. It doesn't have to be on the same day ninety million other people are having a holiday.

— LOUIS BROMFIELD (1896–1956)
American writer

Nobody tries to make the coyotes act like beavers,
or the eagles behave like robins.

— WALKING BUFFALO (1871–1967)
Canadian Stoney Indian

The country is lyric,—the town dramatic. When mingled, they make the most perfect musical drama.

— HENRY WADSWORTH LONGFELLOW *(1807–1882)*
American poet

Where once the craft of working the land and reaping its harvest was passed from father to son, today the torch of knowledge and experience consists of how to get credit cards and fill out tax forms.

— RICHARD W. LANGER, b. 1935
American writer

Earth is here so kind, that just tickle her with a hoe and she laughs with a harvest.

— DOUGLAS JERROLD (1803–1857)
English playwright, author

*I suppose the pleasure of country life lies really in the eternally renewed
evidence of the determination to live.*

— VITA SACKVILLE-WEST (1892–1962)
English writer

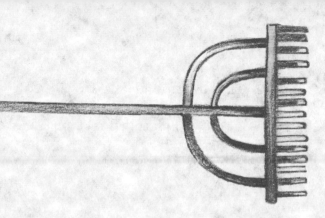

The family farm, the small farmers, are the dropouts that stayed in
when the rest of America dropped out.

— RACHEL PEDEN, b. 1937
American author

To plow is to pray—to plant is to prophesy, and the harvest answers and fulfills.

— R. G. INGERSOLL (1833–1899)
American lecturer, lawyer

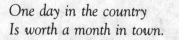

One day in the country
Is worth a month in town.
— CHRISTINA GEORGINA ROSSETTI (1830–1894)
    English poetess

My cow milks me.

— RALPH WALDO EMERSON *(1803–1882)*
American essayist, poet

The wind was blowing, but not too hard, and everyone was so happy and gay for it was only twenty degrees below zero and the sun shone.

— LAURA INGALLS WILDER (1896–1957)
American writer

I believe the first receipt to farm well is to be rich.

— SYDNEY SMITH *(1771–1845)*
English clergyman, author

Five crows, frock-coated in dignity, have arrived and sit upright and still in a bough. One thinks, "Oh, beloved symbols of New England" or "Drat those birds," depending on whether one is planning a poem or a cornfield.

— RICHARD F. MERRIFIELD, b. 1905
American writer

It was time to leave New York and return to civilization. It was time to move back to the country.

— MICHAEL HARWOOD AND MARY DURANT, *b. 1938, b. 1941*
American authors

For man's need of land is not only for food and shelter but equally for occasional solitude.

— RACHEL PEDEN, b. 1937
American author

A man who owns land and lives on it eventually creates his own self-portrait in the fields.

— VANCE BOURJAILY, b. 1922
American writer

God made the country, and man made the town.
— WILLIAM COWPER (1731–1800)
British poet

Until I moved to the mountains, the coming of spring had been a gradual and painless thing, like developing a bust.

— BETTY MACDONALD (1908–1958)
American author

My grandfather on my father's side arose in the dark, arrived in the fields before light, and dozed on the plow handles until it was light enough to work. It was a habit he was never disciplined enough to break. When he was well into his seventies, he was still getting up before daybreak, sitting around on imaginary plowshares, and looking for some new ground to work.

— JOHN BASKIN, b. 1941
American writer

They were just like all the people that they were trying to get away from, except that in the country they had allowed their personalities to expand.

— JOHN P. MARQUAND (1896–1960)
American writer

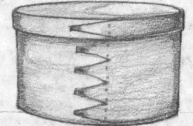

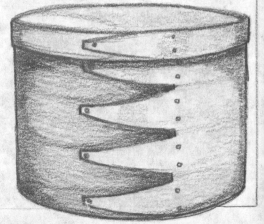

I like a man who likes to see a fine barn as well as a good tragedy.

— RALPH WALDO EMERSON (1803–1882)
American essayist, poet

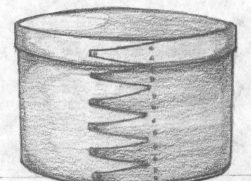

The advantage of living on a farm is that cows and chickens don't come in and urge you to play bridge when you'd rather read.

— EVAN ESAR, b. 1899
American humorist

"Had a big windstorm here yesterday," said the forlorn native of Western Kansas to the solicitous traveler, "that blew away my house, my wife, and my three children." That's terrible! But why aren't you out looking for them?" "No use to look for them. Wind'll change next week and they'll come back."

— B. A. BOTKIN (1901–1975)
Folklore compiler

The land dripped with richness, the fat cows and pigs gleaming against green, and, in the smaller holdings, corn standing in little tents as corn should, and pumpkins all about.

— JOHN STEINBECK (1902–1968)
American author

Farming is a very fine thing, because you get such an unmistakable answer as to whether you are making a fool of your-self, or hitting the mark.

— GOETHE (1749–1832)
German poet

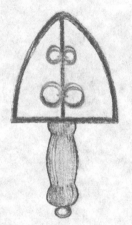

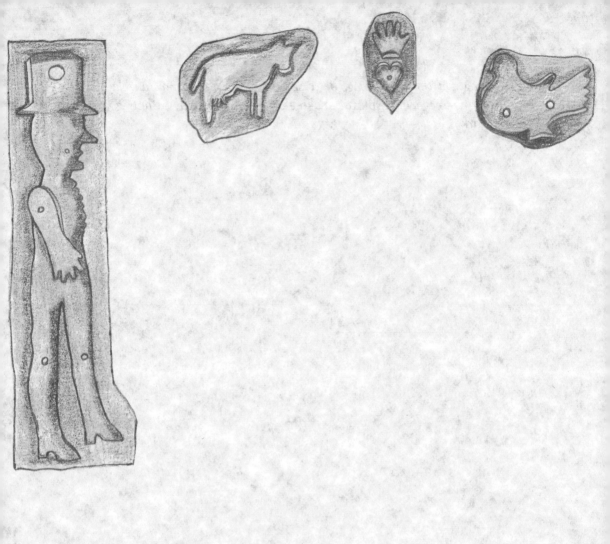

Most of the handbooks of country living are written by flabby men at
the Waldorf-Astoria, who lie in bed and dictate them to secretaries.

— S. J. PERELMAN (1904–1979)
American humorist

Liked the rural life, too, although Dad got struck by lightning in the north forty and for six years afterwards when asked his name could only say the word "kleenex."

— WOODY ALLEN, b. 1935
American author, playwright, comedian

In the long history of man, all of us Americans are but a moment removed from the plains, the mountains, the rivers, the farms, the villages—and from our own frontier.

— THE NATIONAL GEOGRAPHIC SOCIETY (*founded 1888*)

There's nothin' better in the world than gettin' up before daylight and goin' and seein' the sun come up. Nothin' better than bein' in the field when the sun comes down, comin' in by the light of the tractor every night.

— STUDS TERKEL, b. 1912
American author, interviewer

Hills are always more beautiful than stone buildings, you know.
— WALKING BUFFALO (1871–1967)
Canadian Stoney Indian

A wild bird in a thicket and a man in a house cannot be neighbors.

— HENRY BEETLE HOUGH, *b. 1896*
American editor

You can shave a peg to save a nickle and ruin a 50-cent jackknife.
— ARTHUR LITTEER (1904–1973)
Dairy farmer

The mountains are all right, I guess, but they sure do block the view.

— PETER BERGLUND, b. 1916
Retired Saskatchewan farmer

In the country Sunday is the day on which you do exactly as much work as you do on other days but feel guilty all of the time you are doing it because Sunday is a day of rest.

— BETTY MACDONALD (1908–1958)
American author

Command large fields, but cultivate small ones.

— VIRGIL (70 B.C.–19 B.C.)
Roman poet

. . . Ten years ago the deficit on my farm was about a hundred dollars; but by well-designed capital expenditure, by drainage and by greater attention to details, I have got it into the thousands.

— STEPHEN LEACOCK (1869–1944)
Canadian essayist and humorist

I went to the woods because I wished to live deliberately, to front only the essential facts of life, and see if I could not learn what it had to teach, and not, when I came to die, discover that I had not lived.

— HENRY DAVID THOREAU (1817–1862)
American author, philosopher

The everlasting appeal of a sparkling stream and a bamboo pole is not confined to small boys playing hooky.

— MARJORIE BLANCHARD, b. 1946
American writer

By December the valley people are really dug in for winter. Wood is piled high in sheds, cabbages and pots are binned in the cellars, and squash and apples are stored.

— GLADYS TABER (1899–1980)
American author

If one is not in a hurry, even an egg will start walking.

— ETHIOPIAN PROVERB

One morning we ran into a neighbor at the store and she asked brightly, "What was it at your house?"

"Fourteen below," we replied.

Her face fell. "We had minus twelve," she said, and you could see that her day was ruined.

— RICHARD KETCHUM, b. 1922
American writer

Live within your harvest.
— PERSIAN PROVERB

There was nothing else to see but the endless, low white land and the huge pale sky, and the horses' blue shadows blotting the sparkle from the snow.

— LAURA INGALLS WILDER (1867–1957)
American writer

A gentleman farmer is one who has time to read all the government literature on farming.

— EVAN ESAR, *b. 1899*
American humorist

The number of pigs dying of heart ail-ments has doubled in recent years. Apparently the stress of adjusting to modern farming methods is too much for them.

— GERMAN RESEARCH SOCIETY

The best part of living in the country is the people you don't meet.

— EVAN ESAR, b. 1899
American humorist

If you are afraid of blood, sweat, and tears, a constant pain in your sacro-iliac, athlete's foot, poison ivy and 3 A.M. rising, better stick to the city, my friend. If you're not afraid of all these things, better stick to the city anyway.

— ROBERT BENCHLEY (1899–1945)
American humorist

The history of a nation is only the history of its villages written large.

— WOODROW WILSON (1856–1924)
American President

Here in these woods areas, you have a reputation. A dishonest person can't survive in the community. A man lives by his reputation and by his honesty and by his ambition to work.

— JOHN MCPHEE, *b. 1931*
American author

To enjoy living in the country requires the mind of a philosopher, the feeling of an artist, the soul of a poet—and a good station wagon.

— EVAN ESAR, b. 1899
American humorist

Every man looks at his woodpile with a kind of affection.

— HENRY DAVID THOREAU (1817–1862)
American writer

We have learned to be chary of roads; they mean people, and commotion, and lack of peace.

— HERBERT JACOBS, b. 1903
American writer

The woodchopper, by using the force of gravity, lets the planet chop his stick.

— RALPH WALDO EMERSON (1803–1882)
American essayist, poet

Farming is about twenty per cent agriculture and eighty percent mending something that has got busted.

— E. B. WHITE, b. 1899
American humorist, author

Outside of a spring lamb trotting into a slaughterhouse, there is nothing in the animal kingdom as innocent and foredoomed as the new purchaser of a country place.

— S. J. PERELMAN (1904–1979)
American humorist

A farm is a place of opportunity simultaneous with obligation.

— RACHEL PEDEN, b. 1937
American author

A good farmer is nothing more nor less than a handy man with a sense of humus.

— E. B. WHITE, b. 1899
American author, humorist

We found that a very old house in the country does not encourage sitting under blossoming apple trees and sipping tall, cool drinks or strolling among the wild flowers in the woods. When we were in the yard, we were mowing or planting roses by the picket fence or trimming the lilacs.

— GLADYS TABER (1899–1980)
American writer

When tillage begins, other arts follow. The farmers therefore are the founders of human civilization

— DANIEL WEBSTER (1782–1852)
American statesman

*Even if a farmer intends to loaf, he gets up in time
to get an early start.*

— E. W. HOWE (1853–1937)
American publisher, writer

The farther we get away from the land, the greater our insecurity.

— HENRY FORD (1863–1947)
American automobile manufacturer

Many eyes go through the meadow,
but few see the flowers in it.

-- RALPH WALDO EMERSON (1803–1882)
 American essayist, poet

No man ever really owns the land; it belongs to itself and a farmer should regard it with more of humility than a sense of ownership.

— RACHEL PEDEN, b. 1937
American author

One swallow, so we say, doesn't make a spring, But a dozen of them—with a few robins in for good measure—certainly do.

— JOHN BURROUGHS (1837–1921)
American nature writer

To a person uninstructed in natural history, his country or sea-side stroll is a walk through a gallery filled with wonderful works of art, nine-tenths of which have their faces turned to the wall.

— THOMAS HUXLEY (1825–1895)
English biologist

I was raised on the farm. My mother said that milking cows would make my fingers strong for playing the piano.

— MARLA STUTZ, *b. 1943*
Country dweller

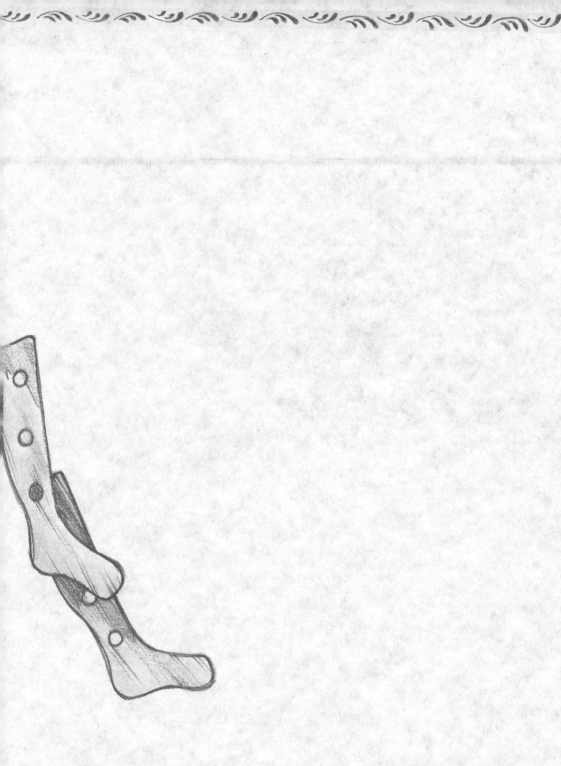

. . . I must say, that one cause of the sad fact why idiocy more prevails among farmers than any other class of people, is owing to their undertaking the mending of rotten rail-fences in warm, relaxing spring weather.

— HERMAN MELVILLE *(1819–1891)*
American novelist

Worm or beetle—drought or tempest—on a farmer's land may fall,
Each is loaded full 'o ruin, but a mortgage beats 'em all.

— WILL CARLETON (1845–1912)
American poet

A blizzard is a beautiful thing. As the drifts pile up, topping the picket fence, I can see from my window the meadow brimmed with silver.

— GLADYS TABER (1899–1980)
American author

I just want to live where I can stretch my arms without hitting someone else in the face.

— THE NATIONAL GEOGRAPHIC SOCIETY *(founded 1888)*